FIRST
PEOPLES
of NORTH
AMERICA

THE PEOPLE AND CULTURE OF THE
MANDAN

TATIANA RYCKMAN
RAYMOND BIAL

Cavendish
Square

New York

Published in 2017 by Cavendish Square Publishing, LLC
243 5th Avenue, Suite 136, New York, NY 10016

First Edition

Website: cavendishsq.com

This publication represents the opinions and views of the author based on his or her personal experience, knowledge, and research. The information in this book serves as a general guide only. The author and publisher have used their best efforts in preparing this book and disclaim liability rising directly or indirectly from the use and application of this book.

CPSIA Compliance Information: Batch #CW17CSQ

All websites were available and accurate when this book was sent to press.

Library of Congress Cataloging-in-Publication Data

Names: Ryckman, Tatiana, author. | Bial, Raymond, author.
Title: The people and culture of the Mandan / Tatiana Ryckman and Raymond Bial.
Other titles: Mandan.
Description: New York : Cavendish Square Publishing, [2017] | Series: First peoples of North America | Includes bibliographical references and index.
Identifiers: LCCN 2016033895 (print) | LCCN 2016034175 (ebook) | ISBN 9781502622495 (library bound) | ISBN 9781502622501 (ebook)
Subjects: LCSH: Mandan Indians--Juvenile literature.
Classification: LCC E99.M2 B53 2016 (print) | LCC E99.M2 (ebook) | DDC 978.400497/522--dc23
LC record available at https://lccn.loc.gov/2016033895

Editorial Director: David McNamara
Editor: Kristen Susienka
Copy Editor: Rebecca Rohan
Associate Art Director: Amy Greenan
Production Coordinator: Karol Szymczuk
Photo Research: J8 Media

Printed in the United States of America

ACKNOWLEDGMENTS

This book would not have been possible without the generous help of many individuals and organizations that have dedicated themselves to honoring the customs of the Mandan.

We would like to thank the staff at Cavendish Square Publishing and all who contributed to finding photos and other materials for publication. Finally, we would like to thank our families and friends for their encouragement and support along our writing journey.

CONTENTS

Amy Mossett, a
Mandan-Hidatsa
woman, is dressed in
traditional clothing.

AUTHORS' NOTE

At the dawn of the twentieth century, Native Americans were thought to be a vanishing race. However, despite four hundred years of warfare, deprivation, and disease, Native Americans have persevered. Countless thousands have lost their lives, but over the course of this century and the last, the populations of Native tribes have grown tremendously. Even as America's First People struggle to adapt to modern Western life, they have also kept the flame of their traditions alive—the languages, religions, stories, and the everyday ways of life. An exhilarating renaissance in Native American culture is now sweeping the continent from coast to coast.

The First Peoples of North America books depict the social and cultural life of the major nations, from the early history of Native peoples in North America to their present-day struggles for survival and dignity. Historical and contemporary photographs of traditional subjects, as well as period illustrations, are blended throughout each book so that readers may gain a sense of family life in a tipi, a hogan, longhouse, or in houses today.

No single book can comprehensively portray the intricate and varied lifeways of an entire tribe, or nation. We only hope that young people will come away with a deeper appreciation for the rich tapestry of Native American culture—both then and now—and a keen desire to learn more about these first Americans.

Artist George Catlin painted this image of a Mandan Okipa ceremony in the nineteenth century.

CHAPTER ONE

A CULTURE BEGINS

Lone Man came to the Heart River, where there was a hill nearby shaped like a heart ... this he decided was to be the "heart of the world," and this hill is still holy to our people.

—Scattercorn, Mandan woman

When European settlers first traveled across North America in the 1700s, they met a tribe along the Upper Missouri River called the Mandan. Nearly four thousand tribespeople were living on the plains of central North Dakota in **earth lodges**, where they welcomed weary travelers. The Mandan settled in villages and developed an **agrarian society**. European traders and trappers who traveled along the Missouri were welcomed into the Mandan villages and their warm dwellings, where they learned about the tribes and kept detailed notes about what they learned.

Origins

Speaking a **Siouan** language, the Mandan may have originally lived in the forests of the lower Missouri River Valley—far from the northern prairies that would become their home. Some scholars believe they may have originated as far away as present-day Ohio. Traditionally, they referred to themselves as Numakaki, meaning "People." Like other Native American tribes, they raised corn and other crops, and they hunted and gathered. As early as 1000 CE, the Mandan may have begun to migrate northwestward, up the Missouri River. Eventually, they settled along the upper Missouri near the mouth of the White River on the **Great Plains** in present-day South Dakota. Sometime after 1150, they were pushed farther upriver when the ancestors of the Arikara migrated into the region. They moved into present-day North Dakota and settled along the Heart River in an area known as the Big Bend of the Missouri.

For a while, the Mandan lived in separate northern and southern groups. However, by 1600, all the Mandan people lived in the territory along the upper Missouri near the mouth of the Heart River. There they planted corn, beans, and squash in the rich soils of the river bottoms and hunted buffalo on the windswept plains. Unlike the nomadic tribes of the Great Plains, who lived in **tipis**, the Mandan established permanent villages of earth lodges clustered around a sacred

The Mandan painted great works of art on buffalo skins and other animal hides.

plaza. These earth lodges of the Mandan and those of the neighboring Hidatsa were large enough to accommodate up to sixty people. During the brutally cold winters, there was even room for their horses. The lodges were dug into the earth, as deep as 4 feet (1.2 meters). A sturdy timber frame was constructed and covered with heavy layers of soil and sod. Naturally insulated, the lodges were warm during the worst blizzards of winter and cool through the hottest days of summer. Overgrown with grass, the roofs were so strong that people could sit on them during pleasant weather.

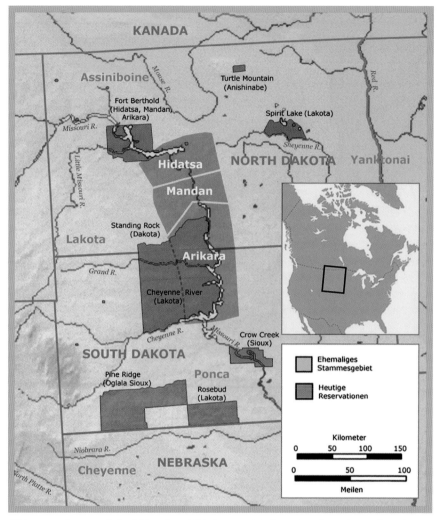

This map shows original Mandan, Hidatsa, and Arikara territory (green) and where reservations are today (orange).

Much is known about the Mandan because they frequently had visitors who wrote detailed accounts and made drawings and paintings vividly depicting their way of life. These portrayals included daily life and religious activities, notably the sacred **Okipa ceremony**. The first known contact with Europeans occurred in 1738 when Pierre de la Vérendrye, a French explorer on a mission for the Canadian Fur Company, ventured into Mandan territory. He received a friendly welcome into the earth lodges. When Meriwether Lewis and William Clark stayed with the Mandan during their epic **expedition**, which began in 1804, the explorers made extensive notes about Mandan customs. During the 1830s, artists George Catlin and Karl Bodmer journeyed up the Missouri River and painted the Mandan.

However, there were negatives to outside influences—most notably, visitors who brought diseases. In 1837, the American Fur Company established Fort Clark near the villages. A few months later, a devastating smallpox **epidemic** struck the villages. Of an estimated population of 1,600 people, only about 135 remained by October of that year.

The surviving Mandan joined the Hidatsa. In 1845, the Mandan and the Hidatsa moved to Fort Berthold in western North Dakota where they lived in a common settlement known as Like-a-Fishhook Village. In 1862, the Arikara also joined them at the fort. In 1871, the Fort Berthold **Reservation** was formally established there for the three tribes.

The Mandan and the Land

For hundreds of years, the Mandan made their home along the Missouri and the other rivers that branched through the prairies of North Dakota. To the east, the land was flat. However, as one ventured westward, the terrain began to roll in waves of grass, broken by ridges and punctuated with lakes and marshes, known as sloughs. Clumps of trees were scattered on the low hills, and woods fringed the banks of every river. To the southwest lay a jagged region of barren, impassable, yet strikingly beautiful canyons and rock formations known as the badlands.

In the Missouri River Valley where the Mandan lived, the land and the climate were more favorable than that of the open prairie. Two hundred to four hundred feet (61 to 121 m) lower than the surrounding plains, the river bottoms provided shelter from the weather, especially from the unrelenting winds and fierce winter blizzards. As the Missouri River meandered through the floodplain and overflowed the banks with spring runoff, it enriched the soil with silt. When cleared of brush, this soil was as fertile as any on earth. Rainfall was often scant on the high plains overlooking the valley, but the villagers always had an abundant source of water in the nearby river. The growing season was short, but the Mandan developed a tough kind of corn, just 3 or 4 feet (0.9 or 1.21 m) tall, that matured in only sixty to seventy days. Thick stands of willows and cottonwoods flourished, along with hardwoods such as burr oak, elm, green ash, box elder, and hackberry. These trees provided the Mandan with a ready supply of firewood and timber for building lodges, palisaded walls, and other village structures.

To avoid the spring flooding, the Mandan situated their main lodges on somewhat higher ground. This was usually on the northwest bank because nearly all the tributaries in the Dakotas, such as the Knife River, flowed from the west into the Missouri River. Occasionally, they established their villages on the high plains. However, the Mandan usually selected two bluffs, or terraces, above the floodplain as the building

The People and Culture of the Mandan

sites for their winter and summer villages. The winter village was located about 35 to 45 feet (10.7 to 13 m) above the river and the summer village was about 80 to 100 feet (24 to 30.5 m) above the floodplain. The higher land usually had no trees, just streaming grasses, and little protection from the wind. During the worst months of winter, the Mandan moved into lodges on the floodplain where they had better shelter and firewood was closer at hand. In early spring, when the snow melted and the river began to rise again, the Mandan moved into their villages on the bluffs.

The Mandan caught turtles in the rivers near their home.

The three elevations—floodplains, bluffs, and the high plains—offered an abundance of animals and plants for food and materials for clothing and shelter. Women and children gathered wild fruit, such as chokecherries, buffalo berries, plums, and grapes. They dug prairie turnips, which came to be known as Indian potatoes. They sometimes raided the nests of field mice for the large beans they had collected there. The men hunted deer, elk, and antelope, but mostly they relied on buffalo (officially known as bison). During the summer, they pursued buffalo herds on the plains. During the intensely cold winter, they stalked the shaggy animals that wandered among the trees along the river where they were sheltered from the cold winds. In the wide river, the Mandan caught catfish and sturgeon, along with turtles. They gathered mussels from the muddy bottom in the low water along the banks.

Although their northern home may seem harsh because of the bitterly cold winters and scant rainfall, the Mandan wisely made use of the land and prospered there for many centuries.

The Mandan Creation Story

As weary travelers sat around the Mandan's flickering fire, they listened to stories about the origin of the Mandan. One of the stories explains how two heroes, First Creator (Coyote) and Lone Man, made the world. Parts of this creation story gave rise to further stories, and in some of the tales Coyote corrects the mistakes of the original creation. Here is one version of that original creation story:

> In the beginning, the earth was covered by water and veiled in darkness. Lone Man wondered who he was and retraced his steps on the water to find out. He met First Creator and learned that First Creator was his father.

They wanted to improve the earth and found a small duck. They asked how she was able to find food in all that water and darkness. She told them that there was food far below the surface. To prove it, the duck dove into the depths of the water and returned with a little ball of soil.

When they saw the soil, First Creator and Lone Man exclaimed, "If this soil keeps the duck alive, it must also be good for other creatures. Let us create land out of this soil. Plants may then grow on this land to sustain the animals."

They each took a little soil to form separate portions of the world. Lone Man chose the northern part and First Creator took the southern area. They left a space in between for the Missouri River. Agreeing to compare their results afterwards, they eagerly plunged into their work.

First Creator formed rolling hills and wide valleys filled with timber. He scooped out low ground for lakes and streams. Once he had shaped the land, he made the animals—buffalo, deer, antelope, elk, and other creatures—that would provide the people with food, clothing, and shelter. Lone Man devoted himself to making low, flat prairies dotted with marshes. He created other animals—the beaver, muskrat, and otter—that like to live in the water. He also

The Great Plains landscape of the Mandan territory consisted of grasslands and endless blue skies.

The People and Culture of the Mandan

made cattle of many colors with long horns and tails.

When they were finished, First Creator and Lone Man met to compare their work. First Creator stated boldly, "Your creations do not meet my approval. Your level prairie does not offer any protection from the wind. My land has hills and bluffs where people and animals may find shelter. They may also note landmarks. Your prairie has no special features, and people will easily lose their way. My rivers and streams run with clear refreshing water, while the still water of your marshes is not safe to drink."

Lone Man responded, "I created the land and animals that I thought would be most useful to people, and I cannot change them now. So, let people first make use of what you have made. When these creatures are gone, then people may use the animals I have created."

So it was agreed. They blessed their creations and then parted. Over the generations, people hunted the buffalo and other animals, and grew corn in their fields. Over time, as the buffalo disappeared, they came to raise cattle.

This creation myth is both the basis of the Mandan culture and a haunting forecast of the tribe's future.

The Mandan left the fertile land of the Ohio valley for the plains of North Dakota, where travelers, though welcome, overhunted buffalo and scared them away with new methods of transportation, like horses and machines. These travelers also brought disease that killed off the Natives while rats, which had traveled on ships from Europe, ate the Mandan's stores of crops. Though there are still Mandan tribespeople in North Dakota today, their numbers have dropped to only a few hundred and they have joined with other neighboring tribes—the Hidatsa and the Arikara—to keep their communities alive. This group is known today as the Three **Affiliated** Tribes.

The Mandan lived in earth lodges such as these.

We Indian people loved our gardens, just as a mother loves her children.

—Buffalo Bird Woman

BUILDING A CIVILIZATION

Drought and unpredictable weather in the 1200s forced migration among different tribes. The Mandan and Hidatsa shared a language and neighboring towns, while the Arikara people began trading and working with the Mandan out of necessity. Both tribes relied on farming, and the lack of rain forced the tribes to rely on each other while also putting them in competition for fertile land and crops. Trade between these groups became so common that after the 1300s, their pottery, tools, and weapons began to look the same.

First Settlements

Increased migration and contact between tribes also meant increased violence, and in the 1300s, villages were built with fortifications to protect the tribes from potential attackers. The Mandan made their home at the center of trade along the banks of the upper Missouri River. Traditionally, there were twenty to more than one hundred lodges in each village.

George Catlin visited the Mandan. This is his take on one Mandan village.

When explorer Pierre Vérendrye visited in 1738, the Mandan had nine villages. At the time of Lewis and Clark's arrival, they inhabited the two villages of Mitutahank and Ruptare. Both villages were situated below the mouth of the Knife River, and both have since been buried under its waters. The two villages were composed of forty to fifty circular earth lodges, each ranging from 40 to 60 feet (12 to 18 m) in diameter.

Whether political, economic, or religious, all Mandan activities were focused on the village. The village was composed mainly of a cluster of earth lodges, but unlike the Hidatsa, the Mandan also had a central plaza and a large medicine lodge that could be more than 90 feet (27 m) long. In the center of this plaza was the so-called Big Canoe, a circular wall of cottonwood planks enclosing a red-painted cedar pole that represented Lone Man. It was believed that Lone Man had once built a similar wall to save the people from a flood. At the north end of the plaza stood the medicine lodge where people gathered for sacred ceremonies. The lodges of the most influential and powerful families were situated nearest to the center of the village. About ten people lived in each permanent lodge. Soon after moving north, the Mandan began to protect their villages with ditches and palisaded walls. When they first encountered Europeans, most of their villages were protected by such fortifications, or occasionally by ravines, cliffs, or high riverbanks.

People often traveled between the villages, including those of the nearby Hidatsa, to trade and visit. Hosts and their guests gathered around the fire to talk and share good food. Dancers and singers also went to other villages to conduct religious ceremonies. The Mandan traditionally welcomed people into their villages, which helped Lewis and Clark when they journeyed up the Missouri River. Sheheke, or Big White, the chief of the lower village of Mitutahank, told explorers, "Our wish is to be at peace with you … If we eat, you shall eat; if we starve, you must starve also."

In the fertile bottomlands around their villages, the Mandan carefully tended their fields of corn, beans, and squash. They also grew a little tobacco, but corn was by far their most important crop. As fall approached, other tribes and traders came to the villages, bringing

The Mandan grew many crops, including prized corn, beans, and squash.

a variety of goods. At the height of the season, the Cree, Cheyenne, Assiniboine, Crow, and even the Teton Sioux with whom the Mandan often warred traded with these farming people. Anything—even dried meat, swift horses, musical instruments, and iron kettles—was traded for the Mandan's precious corn.

The Mandan used bull-boats made of buffalo hides stretched over a wooden frame to paddle goods and people across rivers. They relied on dogs to pull sled-like **travois** until they acquired horses around 1745. The Mandan then used horses to transport goods, as well as to carry men into battle or on buffalo hunts.

House and Home

When the Mandan still lived in the lower Missouri River Valley, they built rectangular lodges that could be as large as 35 by 75 feet (10.7 by 23 m). Most were considerably smaller, however. First, the ground was dug out and a framework of rounded timbers was constructed. Then, soil from the floor was piled around the outside of the lodge and the roof was covered with thatch. Around 1500, the Mandan began to cover the entire lodge with soil and sod. At this time, the Mandan living in the southern area also began to build their lodges in a circular shape. Between 1550 and 1600, the northern group also began to adopt the circular shape, although they still used rectangular buildings for their medicine lodges.

Women were primarily responsible for designing, building, and maintaining the earth lodges. Men might help by placing the heaviest timbers, but the women owned the lodges. Four vertical timbers placed about 15 to 18 feet (4.5 to 5.5 m) apart and four horizontal timbers formed the main structure. Twelve shorter forked posts about 8 feet (2.4 m) tall were then placed around the circumference of this frame. These twelve posts supported the rafters that extended to the smoke hole at the top of the roof. Vertical posts ran down to the ground from these posts to form the log walls. Willow branches were lashed horizontally over the framework and covered with dry grass and layers of sod and loose soil. The Mandan believed that their earth lodges were alive. They prayed to their dwellings and decorated them with cloth offerings.

During the winter, people left these earth lodges, formed seasonal communities in sheltered valleys, and moved into smaller lodges. Built by the women, these dwellings were similar to the earth lodges. Four tall forked tree trunks, about 12 feet (3.7 m) in length, were pounded into the ground. Crossbeams were then lashed to these logs to form a structure that supported the poles of the slanted roof. The structure was covered with soil. In the early 1900s, Mandan tribe member Buffalo Bird Woman recalled her younger days when people had cut trees for making winter homes: "Axes were ringing in all directions. Here and there two women would be cutting trees near each other and a tree would threaten to fall on one of them. The cutter could be heard crying, 'Look out!' Everybody was busy."

Earth lodges had a single low door. Just inside the door was the *widá-daktsuti*, a partition of upright wooden posts that kept the wind from blowing directly into the earth lodge. Inside the earth lodge, there was a fire pit in the center for cooking and heating, with the smoke hole in the roof directly above. Hides were smoke-dried near the fire. There were no windows—the only light came from the doorway and the smoke hole. During rainstorms, the smoke hole was often covered with a round buffalo-bull boat. The bed of the most honored man who lived in the dwelling was located in the central area near the fire. Facing the door, the place of honor, known as *atuka*, was also situated in the central area.

The lodge interior was divided into compartments—one area for horses and firewood, another for sleeping, and an open center for eating and socializing. The *atuti*,

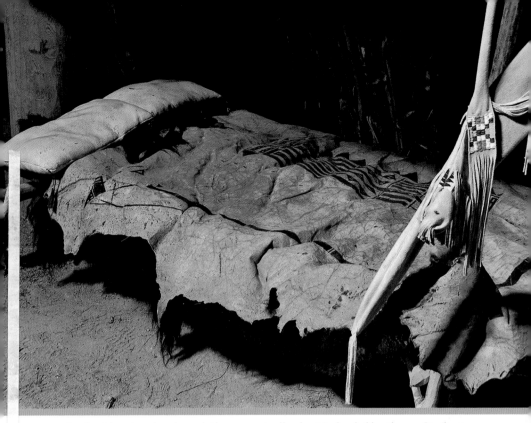

As the Mandan developed, they eventually slept in beds like these. Similar to beds today, they are raised and complete with a pillow and blanket.

or perimeter of the lodge, served as a storage space for firewood and a corral where favorite horses were sheltered from enemies or severe storms. Sleeping compartments were also arranged around the outer wall. Within the lodge, a raised platform was used for preparing and serving meals, as well as food storage. The Mandan stored dried beans, corn, squash, and various roots in deep storage pits dug into the dirt floors of the lodges and along the paths between the lodges. The stores of dried food nourished the people during the cold months. These pits were opened every four days to remove food, then closed again. The lodge owner's sacred bundles, or medicine bags, were kept at a shrine.

Family was very important to the Mandan. This buffalo hide is decorated with symbols representing a family or clan.

The People and Culture of the Mandan

Over time, the Mandan adopted the ways of the explorers and settlers who came into their country. Around 1870, people began to move into log cabins. Often the cabin had two rooms, one of which was inhabited by the older members of the family and the other by the younger people.

Creating a Culture

In Mandan society, people belonged to the clan of their mother. Children were brought up in their mother's, not their father's, lodge, and when a son was ready for marriage, he went to join his bride in her lodge. Consequently, the earth lodges were managed by the women who lived in them.

Women, in fact, did most of the work in the village. The men were responsible for religious practices, defense, and hunting. They occasionally helped their wives cut the large logs for the lodges. Others left the work entirely to the women. Women—who built the houses, raised the crops, tanned the hides, and made all the clothing—enriched their families. Men undertook few chores and relied on the hardworking women. An industrious woman was regarded by the men as a source of wealth and prestige. Through their work, women achieved high status and respect in the community.

A man passed through seven major societies, or lodges, as he grew older. When he was between eighteen to twenty years of age, a young man could enter the first or lowest society, the Fox order. To join, he first had to purchase the rights of a member of this society. He could then progress through the other societies. No one younger than fifty was allowed to enter the Buffalo Bull society, the highest attainment.

Originally, there were thirteen Mandan clans. Each clan was organized according to kinship. Clan members elected their own leaders, usually older men who had proven themselves as hunters and demonstrated a genuine concern for the welfare of the clan. Each clan was responsible for its own members, including orphans and old people. The clan had its own sacred bundles, and members gathered in their leader's home to plan important ceremonies. The clan also helped with funerals and avenged the deaths of its members.

Village leaders were chosen from among those who owned sacred bundles. The two key leaders were the war chief and the peace chief, each of whom was chosen from different clans. The peace chief was responsible for daily affairs and ceremonies. To become a chief, a man first had to lead a war party. He also had to discover and kill an enemy while not leading a war party. Finally, he had to own a white buffalo robe for some time.

The Mandan were a deeply religious people whose ceremonies and visions were related to the sacred bundles. The sacred bundles held precious objects, such as eagle skulls. These bundles represented the physical elements of the history of each clan. The Okipa was the most important ceremony of the Mandan. This annual, four-day ceremony recounted their history as a people. It involved fasting and visions. Participants honored Lone Man, who gave the Mandan their religion; Speckled Eagle, who liberated the animals; and the Foolish One, who was exiled from the village because he did not have faith. An individual could acquire power and prestige by participating in an Okipa ceremony.

 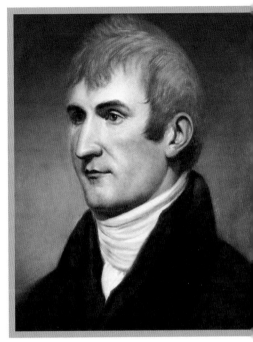

William Clark (*left*) and Merriwether Lewis (*right*) explored the Louisiana Territory, encountering the Mandan along the way.

The Corps of Discovery

The Lewis and Clark expedition, also known as the Corps of Discovery, was dispatched by President Thomas Jefferson to explore land acquired by the United States in the **Louisiana Purchase** and to seek a water route to the Pacific Ocean. As the first snows fell on the prairie, the explorers arrived at the villages on the Knife River on October 26, 1804. There were five villages—two Mandan (Mitutahank and Ruptare) and three Hidatsa—nestled in the Missouri River Valley.

A few British traders and French trappers already lived in the villages, and Hugh McCracken, who worked for the Northwest Fur Company, greeted the explorers. The Mandan had long traded with other Native peoples of the northern plains, and their villages were major trading hubs long before the French and the British began trading for furs.

At the villages, Lewis and Clark hoped to find guides who knew the western lands and interpreters who were familiar with the native peoples living there. Sacagawea, a sixteen-year-old Shoshone woman, and her husband, Toussaint Charbonneau, were living in the villages at the time. Both had a great deal of knowledge. Lewis and Clark came to an agreement with Charbonneau for his services and the help of his wife Sacagawea, who was six months pregnant, in leading the expedition into the lands west of the Knife River.

The Mandan and the Hidatsa welcomed the members of the expedition. Seeking friendship and hoping to spend the winter with their hosts, Lewis and Clark offered gifts, including tools and an iron corn grinder. Given the importance of corn not only as a source of food but in religious ceremonies, the grinder was an especially suitable gift.

Encouraged by the hospitality of the Mandan and Hidatsa, Lewis and Clark decided to build a fort on the east bank of the Missouri River. Fort Mandan was located about 3 miles (4.8 kilometers) east of Mitutahank, the lower Mandan village, and on the same side of the river as Ruptare, which was 5 or 6 miles (8 or 9.6 km) north. Clark chose a site away from all the villages so the fort would not appear to favor any

These sketches from Lewis and Clark's expedition helped later explorers in the area.

one particular community. The men began the work on November 3 and completed the fort about two weeks later. By the end of November, more than 1 foot (0.9 m) of snow had already accumulated on the ground and large chunks of ice floated down the river.

The buffalo herds had already moved south, so the men hunted elk and deer, drying and storing as much meat as possible. Through the winter the game thinned, and the deer and the elk they killed had little flesh on their bones. Hunters often went out in pursuit of game, but their food stores nonetheless dwindled. During the extreme cold, the men needed to eat as much as possible to maintain their strength, but they often went hungry, so Lewis and Clark traded goods for corn. Throughout the winter, the Mandan supplied the

The Mandan, along with many other Native American tribes, hunted buffalo.

1853.

The People and Culture of the Mandan

42.

visitors with food in exchange for trade goods, helping the explorers to survive the brutal North Dakota winter where temperatures often plunged to –45 degrees Fahrenheit (–43 degrees Celsius).

Sheheke and Black Cat, the chiefs of the Mandan villages, often met with Lewis and Clark during the winter. Members of the expedition even took part in some Mandan ceremonies. A steady stream of visitors also came to Fort Mandan to enjoy food and conversation, and to trade for goods. When Lewis and Clark were not socializing and making inquiries, they were busy preparing materials to send to President Jefferson in the spring. Gathering information about the territory was a main purpose of the expedition, and the Mandan were quite helpful in this regard. In 1804, William Clark wrote in his report: "The Mandans are at war with all who make war only, and wish to be at peace with all nations, Seldom the ogressors [sic]." While Clark labored over the preparation of a comprehensive map, Lewis recorded his observations of such things as the native plants and the lifeways of the tribes inhabiting the region.

The expedition spent most of January and February chopping their keelboat and smaller craft out of the ice so that they could make repairs. They ventured out to fell trees to be made into dugout canoes for the next stage of the journey. Toward the end of March, flocks of geese and swans were flying northward above Fort Mandan. The ice on the river began to break up. Buffalo were spotted on the prairie and Sheheke invited the men from Fort Mandan to join in a hunt. It was still very cold, with temperatures hovering just

The People and Culture of the Mandan

below 0°F (–17°C), but fifteen men went on the hunt. That night the temperature plunged to –12°F (–24°C), and the river froze. Three of the expedition's hunters were badly frostbitten. Riding on horseback among the herd, members of the expedition nonetheless killed ten buffalo, five of which were taken back to the fort.

On April 7, 1805, the Mandan bid farewell to the Corps of Discovery. The months of protection and food the Mandan tribe shared with the explorers may be the only reason they survived the harsh North Dakota winter. Lewis and Clark continued their journey up the Missouri River with their guides, Charbonneau and Sacagawea. Sacagawea had been captured from the Shoshone tribe to the west, in present-day Montana, and her knowledge of the Native languages, edible plants, and her connection to the tribes in this region further secured safe passage for the expedition.

Sacagawea's invaluable role on the expedition was representative of the Mandan's culture of hardworking women, who brought their families and clans together. Though the Mandan lived in settlements, where they practiced rituals and grew crops, their appreciation for the earth and their understanding of the natural world helped them when they migrated across a harsh wilderness European settlers had never even seen.

Mandan girls help gather berries, circa 1908.

CHAPTER THREE

It was the women who owned everything ... they owned the homes, they owned the gardens.

—Tillie Walker

LIFE IN A MANDAN VILLAGE

Mandan society was organized into clans, each led by a successful hunter. Every member of the clan did their part to make sure the group could survive and flourish from year to year. Girls were taught to farm and cook, while men were taught to hunt. There was a strong sense of community among clan members, and each clan cared for its own members from birth to death.

Cycle of Life

All cultures have unique rites of passage and traditions that mark the stages one passes through over the course of their lifetime. Some familiar examples include celebrations, such as birthdays, weddings, and funerals. The Mandan tribespeople had their own customs, which marked significant moments in a tribe member's life and helped form a strong community as everyone shared in each other's growth.

Being Born

When she was about to give birth, a woman retired to an earth lodge, preferably the home of her mother. Everyone was sent away from the lodge except an old woman, who remained to assist in the delivery. The dim interior was further darkened by covering the door and part of the smoke hole. A robe was spread on the floor for the woman near two posts that she could grasp during her contractions. If the labor was prolonged, the father's sister prepared an herbal drink for the woman.

As soon as the baby was born, the old woman greased its body and smeared red ocher under the arms, between the legs, and around the neck to ease chafing, as well as on the top of the head. The baby was then wrapped in a piece of soft buckskin and placed in a leather cradle. At night, the baby was taken from the cradle to sleep with its mother.

Ten days later, a feast was held in the lodge, and the baby was named. The parents chose a special friend or relative to host this ceremony. If the father had earned great wealth and prestige in the village, he or his sister named the baby. Otherwise, members

The People and Culture of the Mandan

Artist Karl Bodmer visited the Mandan and painted this scene in the 1800s.

of his clan selected a name. The name related to the sacred bundle of the person giving the name, such as Scattercorn, Pumpkin Blossom, Corn Silk, Sage Woman, or Calf Woman. Family and clan members gave away lavish presents, such as buffalo robes, and the father often gave a horse to a deserving person. The giveaway enhanced the family's social position within the community.

Growing Up

As they grew up, children learned the many complex rituals of the Mandan as well as how to provide for themselves. The mother and other women taught the girls how to construct lodges, manage households, and care for the children. Girls also learned how to grow crops, preserve food, prepare meals, tan hides, and make clothing. The father and other men taught the boys to hunt game and catch fish and the arts of warfare. If a boy was lazy, his mother's brother would chastise him for disgracing the clan. When he was eight or nine years old, a boy was encouraged to learn discipline through fasting. He was also instructed in the Okipa and other important religious ceremonies. Serving as a "grandfather," an older man in the lodge showed the boys how to weave fish traps and to make bows and arrows. He also instructed the boys in games and told stories to all the children. By living in a close-knit society, girls and boys learned to cooperate with others.

Maturing

As they approached adolescence, both girls and boys joined societies. An older sister or mother helped a girl collect enough goods to buy membership into the society. Parents advised boys about buying into a society. Becoming a member of a society required a new set of responsibilities for young people as they progressed to adulthood.

When he fasted during the annual Okipa ceremony, a boy formally became a member of the tribe as a whole. His initial fast, at age eight or nine, was brief, but the duration increased each year, until at age seventeen or eighteen, he fasted for the entire four days of the Okipa. During this ritual, he also dragged buffalo skulls attached to thongs inserted under his skin to show courage and endurance. A girl learned the importance of fasting, too, during such times as when

The Mandan held lively celebrations throughout the year.

her brother went away to make war or raid an enemy camp. It was believed that her sacrifice would bring him good fortune in striking the enemy or capturing horses.

When they had learned the skills of survival and understood the important religious beliefs of the Mandan, young women and men were considered adults who were ready to be married.

Marrying

Although young men and women often courted, families usually arranged the marriages. When a mother observed that her daughter was interested in a certain young man, she discussed the matter with her husband. She then advised her daughter not to marry without a generous exchange of goods. She also emphasized the importance of keeping the sacred bundles in the lodge.

Marriages of common families were largely social occasions with an exchange of presents. Those of the wealthy involved a lavish display of goods and sacred bundles. Families with the most valuable bundles tried to arrange marriages with families who similarly owned important bundles, preferably a family of the same clan as the young man's father. If a young man had proven himself as a hunter and warrior, and his family owned an important bundle, his parents discussed marriage with the parents of a suitable young woman. If the young woman consented, her parents bought a white buffalo robe, which commanded a high price in horses and corn. The young man was then invited into the lodge and an offer of marriage was formally made. The young man was asked to sit with the young woman, and the white buffalo robe was placed over their shoulders. The couple was given food prepared by the mother, and the brothers of the young woman gave horses to the man. The young man then went outside and walked to the top of the lodge. Addressing the sacred bundles of his father, he said that the white buffalo robe had been offered to his father's gods.

The father's sister then came and cared for the robe while the young man gathered all the goods that had been lavished on him. On the date of the actual marriage ceremony these goods, including the white buffalo robe, were prominently displayed. The goods were given away to members of the young man's family as the guests feasted. While people sang and prayed for the good fortune of the couple, the young man and woman offered gifts to the older people. In turn, the older people gave them small articles from their bundles. A figure of the corn plant was then painted on the white buffalo robe.

Dying

An infant who died before receiving a name was wrapped in robes and placed in a tree or buried away from the graves of the other dead. There were no funeral rites because the baby was not yet considered a member of the community. It was believed that the child returned to the Home of the Babies to be reborn at a later time.

When an adult thought that he or she was about to die, relatives were gathered and the dying person was formally dressed and painted. The dying person expressed a wish to be either buried or placed on a scaffold. In early times, most people were buried, often

Scaffolds like this held the bodies of the dead.

on hilltops. The father's clan attended to the body and the funeral rites. These rites included the "sending away of the spirit" on the fourth day, which was undertaken by the women of the clan. The body was placed on a scaffold with the head to the northwest and the feet to the southeast. After four days of mourning, the brothers and sisters divided the goods of the deceased among themselves.

If a man's wife died, the man left her lodge and went to live with members of his own clan. The lodge was either abandoned or taken over by female members of the dead woman's clan. When a married woman with no children lost her husband, she moved into another lodge owned by a woman of her clan. If a woman died leaving young children, her unmarried sisters raised them. If she had no sisters, her parents took care of the grandchildren. If the children had no relatives, the clan still provided for them.

The Mandan believed that the dead gathered in villages in a spirit world. Like the living, they lived in earth lodges, planted fields, hunted game, and participated in religious ceremonies.

Warriors

Like other tribes on the Great Plains, the Mandan were often at war, yet they usually fought only to defend themselves. Although not particularly warlike, Mandan warriors were considered among the bravest of any plains tribe. Beginning in the eighteenth century, they fought against the Sioux and other tribes. They occasionally sent war parties as far as the Rocky Mountains to fight the Blackfeet and as far east as the Red River in present-day Minnesota to attack the Ojibwe. The Mandan traditionally allied with the Hidatsa and the Crow.

A man's social position in the village was based on his courage and skill in battle. A warrior was entitled to wear a wolf's tail on the heel of his moccasin if he had **counted coup**—that is, if he had touched or struck an enemy in battle. If he was the first to touch and kill an enemy in close combat, he was allowed to paint a spiral design around his arm. For killing the second enemy warrior, he could paint his left legging reddish brown. For killing an enemy in an equally matched situation, he could wrap a wolf's tail around each foot. Courageous acts were recognized with a striped design on the arm or an eagle feather worn in the hair. Wooden sticks

This drawing shows a Mandan warrior ready for battle.

The People and Culture of the Mandan

worn in the hair indicated the number of times a warrior had been shot. Some men wore wooden knives to show that they had killed an enemy with these weapons.

When a young man wished to lead his first war party, he sought good medicine from the spirits. Then he offered gifts to his friends and assured them of the power of his medicine and his own ability as a warrior. Large war parties might have as many as four leaders, each of whom carried a medicine pipe on his back. Before they went to war, the men who had agreed to join the war party feasted and danced. As they rode off to engage their foes, each warrior had a whistle around his neck, which he blew upon first sight of the enemy. The war cry was then sounded, and the men attacked.

The Mandan took prisoners only on rare occasions. As soon as a captive had come into the village and eaten corn, he was considered a member of the tribe. However, the women could go out and meet the war party and kill any prisoners before they entered the village. The Mandan took scalps, which they dried and wore proudly. As soon as a triumphant war party returned, the women and children joined them in a Scalp Dance. With their faces and sometimes their bodies painted black, the warriors danced in the medicine lodge for four nights and then in the center of the village. If no Mandan warrior had been killed in the conflict, the celebration might continue for as long as six months.

When going into battle, the Mandan used the same kinds of weapons as other Native peoples of the northern plains: bows and arrows, lances, war clubs, knives, and buffalo-hide shields. They also had their own unique weapon, known as a bow-lance. This was a long bow fitted with a spear point at one end. The bow-lance was lavishly decorated with eagle plumes and other ornaments and used only for ceremonies. Knife blades and points for arrows and lances were originally chipped from stone. Later, the Mandan made points from metal trade goods. The heads of axes and war clubs were also made of stones until steel became available through trade.

Men crafted bows from elm and ash wood and strung them with twisted sinew. Occasionally, they fashioned bows from bone or horn. To make arrows, they selected a straight wooden shaft to which they carefully attached hawk or eagle feathers. They decorated the arrow with a red line that spiraled the length of the shaft. Six- to eight-foot-long (1.8 to 2.4 m long) ash wood lances were fitted with double-edged points and decorated with eagle plumes. The Mandan used several kinds of war clubs. Shields were made by stretching a tough buffalo hide over a wooden frame. The hide was whitened with clay and painted with designs indicating the owner's sacred bundles.

Hunters and Farmers

The Mandan provided food for themselves, according to the cycle of the seasons. The year was measured by a lunar calendar. The name for each month reflected not only the weather but also often a key subsistence activity at that time:

January	Moon of seven cold days
February	Moon of the mating wolves

March	Moon of sore eyes
April	Moon of game; or of the river breakup
May	Moon of sowing; or of flowers
June	Moon of ripe Juneberries
July	Moon of ripe chokecherries
August	Moon of ripe wild plums
September	Moon of ripe corn
October	Moon of the fall of leaves
November	Moon of the freezing rivers
December	Moon of the little cold

Like many Native peoples of North America, the Mandan were excellent farmers. When they moved up the Missouri River into North Dakota, they already had a great deal of agricultural knowledge and experience. Other tribes that migrated onto the sweeping prairies tended to abandon farming. However, even after they became buffalo hunters, the Mandan continued to farm, planting corn, squash, beans, and sunflowers. They also grew a little tobacco, which was used in ceremonies.

Rainfall was often scarce in the region, but the Mandan were experts at raising many varieties of corn that resisted drought. Photographer Edward Curtis, who made many fine portraits of the tribe, observed, "Corn was the chief staple of the Mandan, and was grown in considerable quantities." As the weather began to warm in May, the women cleared the fields. Most fields were situated in the low floodplain of the river, sometimes several miles from the summer village. However, the loose, fertile soil near the river could be easily worked and watered. Rights to these fields were inherited through the women's clans. Fields varied in size. About 1.5 acres (0.6 hectares) was needed to feed each person. Generally, a family cultivated three fields of about 4 or 5 acres (1.6 to 2 ha) each. As the yields declined in some fields, the Mandan cleared new land for farming.

The Mandan also hunted game. By the time Lewis and Clark visited their villages, they were relying almost equally on hunting and farming as sources of food. Men hunted deer, elk, antelope, bighorn sheep, occasionally bear, and smaller game, such as beaver, rabbits, ducks, and geese. Antelope was most often hunted by driving a herd into a brush enclosure that narrowed like a funnel. While some hunters guarded the openings, the others pursued the antelope and clubbed them. However, buffalo were their most vital game for meat and hides.

The men hunted panthers, wolves, foxes, and ermine for their plush fur. Wolves and foxes were most often trapped in pitfalls, which were deep holes covered with branches and baited with meat. The men also hunted eagles and other birds of prey for their feathers. To catch these birds, they traveled to the badlands. There, they dug a pit, covered it with branches, and scattered meat over the branches as bait. The hunter hid in the pit and waited patiently until an eagle or a hawk lit on the branches. The man would grab the bird, pull it into the pit, and quickly kill it. He then waited for another bird.

Buffalo were hunted seasonally and throughout the year when the herds happened to wander near the

Buffalo meat was essential to the Mandan way of life for many centuries.

villages. The Mandan did not make long journeys in pursuit of buffalo. Following the Buffalo Dance in the Okipa ceremony, the people went on their first hunt of the season under the direction of the Soldier Band. The men who owned buffalo skulls in their sacred bundles managed the hunt and the rituals that were held before they swooped down upon the herd. The hunters surrounded a small group of buffalo and killed every animal in an effort not to alarm the entire herd. The carcasses were butchered on the open prairie. The hunters immediately ate the choice parts, such as the heart and the tongue, which would spoil quickly. The horses were then laden with fresh meat and taken back to the village. Women were responsible for preserving the meat, most of which was sliced thin and hung on drying racks placed near fires. The rising smoke helped to dry the meat. Women ground up strips of this dried

RECITE

CORN BALLS

INGREDIENTS

2 cups yellow cornmeal

½ cup dried berries (blueberries, chokecherries, or Juneberries)

1 or 2 tablespoons brown sugar or maple syrup

¼ cup lard or vegetable oil

Chop dried berries in blender. Mix cornmeal and berries together. Melt lard or vegetable oil in a frying pan and lightly brown the dry mixture, adding sweetener and a little more lard or vegetable oil, if needed, until the cornmeal has a stiff dough-like consistency. Remove mixture from frying pan and drain on paper towels. Allow mixture to cool, then form into egg-sized balls. The corn balls may be eaten fresh or allowed to dry in the sun for a few hours. Serves four to six people.

Note: Although known as corn balls in English, the Mandan and other plains tribes often rolled this nutritious corn mixture into cylinders about 3 or 4 inches long.

The People and Culture of the Mandan

meat, or **jerky**, to make **pemmican**. The pemmican was stored in rawhide pouches called **parfleches** (par-FLESH-es) and covered with fat. The women also scraped the hides to be used as robes or tanned into buckskin for clothing.

When the ice on the Missouri River broke up in the spring, the carcasses of drowned buffalo floated downstream. The Mandan gathered many of these dead animals, whose flesh was considered better than fresh meat. The meat was usually hung up and allowed to decay, after which it was flavored even more. The Mandan also considered intestines to be good food.

Food Preparation

Green corn, like the sweet corn that is eaten today, was freshly boiled. Corn was also dried for later use in the winter. Squash was sliced and dried as well. One of the Mandan's favorite dishes was made by mixing cornmeal, sunflower meal, and beans with slices of dried squash and pounding them into a paste. Sunflower seeds were also roasted in a pan and then ground into a powder. Mixed with fat and made into small balls, they were carried by warriors as highly nutritious rations.

Many explorers told of eating stews and soups with buffalo meat and one or more vegetables. Except for those dishes made with the decayed meat of drowned buffalo, they found the food to be quite delicious. People lived mainly on the large stores of vegetables supplemented with large quantities of meat.

Women originally cooked in clay pots, but later adopted kettles brought in by traders. Shortly after moving to Like-a-Fishhook Village in 1845, the Mandan abandoned pottery-making altogether. Cooking utensils were often made of bone. For example, a thin portion of buffalo shoulder was made into a knife for slicing squash. Corn and sunflowers were ground with a wooden mortar and pestle. People ate from bowls carved from wood. They used spoons shaped from buffalo horns and ladles made from the horns of bighorn sheep.

Mah-to-toh-pa was the second chief of the Mandan.

The People and Culture of the Mandan

Traditional Garb

The Mandan dressed like other Native peoples living on the Great Plains. During warm weather, men often wore only a breechcloth made of animal skins. The rectangular piece of leather was drawn between the legs and tied around the waist. As winter approached, men usually changed to deerskin leggings, tanned deerskin shirts decorated with porcupine quills, and fringed moccasins. During cold weather, they also wore gloves and moccasins with fur on the inside and wrapped themselves in buffalo robes. Women wore long-sleeved, ankle-length dresses made by sewing the skins of two mountain sheep or deer together at the sides and shoulders. They tied a wide belt around their waists and often attached pieces of hoof to the hem so they hung in the fringe. They wore ankle-high deerskin moccasins and leggings. They often adorned themselves with bead necklaces and earrings.

Men frequently had tattoos on their right breast and upper arms, or sometimes on their forearms and fingers. Women occasionally tattooed themselves as well.

Men and women carefully groomed themselves, paying special attention to their hair. They began each day with a bath, after which they rubbed their bodies with castoreum, a strong-scented oil obtained from the beaver. Men parted their long hair, with one portion combed forward and the other backward. The forward hair was sometimes braided with ornaments. Men also wore their hair cut at nose length and curled upward with a hot stick in much the same manner that people now use curling irons. The hair on the sides hung to the shoulders while the hair at the back usually fell to the waist. Men often separated their hair into tail-like strands, smeared the strands with clay or spruce gum, and tied them with buckskin strings. They frequently adorned their hair with small shells called dentalia. Women simply plaited their hair into two long braids that hung loosely in front of their shoulders.

The Mandan usually dressed plainly. However, for feasts and ceremonies, they painted their bodies with colorful pigments mixed with grease and wore elaborately decorated clothing. For these occasions, they chose embroidered buckskin shirts trimmed in scalps, fur, and feathers, and moccasins covered with quillwork designs. They also wore necklaces of elk teeth, bear claws, and large glass beads. Shirts and leggings were often fringed with antelope or deer hooves. Mandan regalia also included beautifully painted or embroidered robes, bows, quivers, sacred bundles, tobacco pouches, and pipes. Members of different societies wore impressive headdresses made with eagle, hawk, crow, or raven feathers. Sometimes, they preferred a headdress made of polished buffalo horns.

Traditional Crafts

The Mandan crafted many useful objects, such as tools, household goods, and furnishings for their homes. They constructed beds in their lodges by sinking four posts into the earthen floor and lashing cross poles to them about 1 foot (0.3 m) above the ground, with the posts extending about 3 to 4 feet (0.9 to 1.2 m) above the cross poles. They stretched green, or fresh, buffalo hides over this frame to create a boxlike enclosure.

The Mandan traveled in bull-boats like this one.

They stretched hides across the bottom of the bed (at the level of the cross poles) and over the top and at the sides, leaving a small opening in the front. They placed buffalo robes on the springy bottom hide. These spaces were large enough to accommodate several people.

To travel across wide rivers, the Mandan made bull-boats. First, they bent supple willow branches to form a circular frame about 6 feet (1.8 m) in diameter. This frame consisted of two hoops joined together by crosspieces of willow. A green buffalo hide was then stretched over the frame, hair to the inside, and sewed over the rim. Men split a 5-foot-long (1.5 m long) pole and attached this blade to the boat. Paddled from a standing position, the bull-boat turned nearly halfway around with every stroke. Yet heavy loads could be carried in these small, sturdy vessels.

The Mandan made fish traps, known as weirs, by weaving supple willow branches across streams. They fashioned a hoe by lashing the shoulder blade of a buffalo, or occasionally an elk, to a long wooden handle. To make a simple yet handy rake, they attached a deer antler to a wooden handle. They used bones to make scrapers, needles, and awls, all of which were needed to turn animal skins into clothing and other useful articles.

Women softened and shaped the horns of bighorn sheep and buffalo into spoons and ladles. The long wooden stems of these utensils were often decorated with braids of porcupine quills. Women sometimes used wooden bowls but often made their own clay dishes and cooking pots. These dishes and pots were made of black clay hardened by firing in a kiln. Varying in size and shape, the pots held from one quart to several gallons.

The men traded with the Dakota for stone pipes or made their own from black clay or yellow clay painted black. They also occasionally used pipes with wooden bowls lined with stone. The men made long wooden whistles for use by members of the societies. Each whistle had an eagle feather at the end. War whistles were made from the bones of large birds. They also crafted wooden flutes, about 20 inches (51 centimeters) long, with finger holes for the various notes.

The Mandan were renowned for their leatherwork. They crafted leather pouches and bags and sheaths for knives and bows, all of which were painted or embroidered with quills. They also made saddles and lariats of woven rawhide.

The People and Culture of the Mandan

The Mandan especially were noted for their painting on buffalo robes. These pictures depicted battles and other important historical events. These robes were also lavishly decorated with porcupine quills dyed in various colors.

Games and Pastimes

Men, women, and children all loved to play games and take part in the lively betting that accompanied many of them. One of their favorite games was known as *tchung-kee*. Each player had a spear about 6 feet (1.8 m) long, notched and fitted with bunches of colorful feathers. The object of the game was to throw the spear at a ball or stone ring as it rolled over smooth ground.

Besides ball games and guessing games, the Mandan enjoyed horse races, footraces, and mock battles. They usually raced their horses in a circle around the village. As many as twenty men might take part in the footraces that were run over a course about 7 miles (11 km) long. The men paid a fee to enter the archery contests. The object of these competitions was not to shoot accurately but to shoot as many arrows as possible into the air at once. The winner was the one who shot the most arrows.

The women played a game with a finely sewn and decorated leather ball. The object of this game was to bounce the ball alternately on one's foot and knee.

Children often enjoyed a game called *assé* that was played with a dart made from an antler tip fitted with two feathers. They also rolled a wooden disk covered with leather bands and threw spears at it. The child who struck the hoop nearest the center was the winner.

The Mandan created many objects, such as instruments and tools.

Although they might compete vigorously in games, the Mandan were a kind and generous people. Everyone was expected to share their food with others. No one could become chief without giving away many presents. The record of a man's gifts, as well as his heroic deeds in war, were depicted in paintings on a man's robe. If a person expressed a desire for some object, it was given to him immediately. However, a gift of equal value was expected in return. A man could also buy back anything he had given away by returning what he had been offered.

The Mandan extended the same hospitality to visitors. Explorer Vérendrye noted, "Their custom being to feed liberally all who came among them, selling only what was to be taken away." The Mandan were bound to protect strangers. Even an enemy who took refuge in their village was treated kindly. The property of the enemy would not be taken, and he need not worry about being injured or killed.

The Mandan also gathered to sing and play musical instruments, especially flutes and rattles. They often took part in spirited discussions, and many men were renowned orators and fine storytellers. Everyone liked to gather around the glow of the fire on a long winter night to listen to a tale. These stories recounted the Mandan's history and offered lessons about how one could live a good and useful life.

Skilled in both work and games, the Mandan relied on a deep belief system that explained the way the natural world worked and how people should treat one another. These beliefs governed all that the Mandan did, and was part of what helped them gain a reputation for being welcoming to all.

The Mandan were deeply connected to the earth and all living things around them.

CHAPTER FOUR

I finally got admittance to their sacred enclave, and assured them that I was but a man like themselves.

—Edward Curtis about the Mandan

BELIEFS OF THE MANDAN

The Mandan creation story told in the first chapter of this book is just one building block in the belief system of the Mandan people. These beliefs dictated the tribe's daily life, religious ceremonies, and the way they treated the earth. The Mandan were **polytheistic**, meaning they worshipped multiple gods, but these gods worked together. For the Mandan, the First Creator, also called the Lord of Life, created the world and everything in it. First Creator and his son, Lone Man, figure prominently in creation stories. While First Creator made the land, he bestowed great trust on Lone Man, who had the power to mediate between the spirits and people.

Religious Beliefs

Among the important spirits were Rokanka-Tauihanka, who protected people, and Lying Prairie Wolf, an evil but weak spirit, who wandered the land. There was also Ochkih-Hadda, who came to the village, taught many skills to the Mandan, and then vanished. If he appeared in a dream, it was a sign of death. Yet people displayed images of him in their villages.

People revered the sun as the place where First Creator resided. They believed that Old Woman Who Never Dies, a spirit with a white line around her head, lived on the moon. She was very powerful, and the Mandan often made sacrifices to her. She had six children—three sons and three daughters. The first son was the Day, the second was the Sun, and the third was the Night. The first daughter was the Morning Star, or the Woman Who Carries a Bunch of Feathers. The second was the Striped Pumpkin, a star revolving around the North Star. The third daughter was the Evening Star. People believed in other supernatural beings, including animal people and the Thunderbird.

The Mandan believed that a person had four souls: black, brown, clear, and indistinct. Some people believed that upon death the clear soul returned to First Creator. One of the souls went to the villages in the south that were often visited by gods. Another of

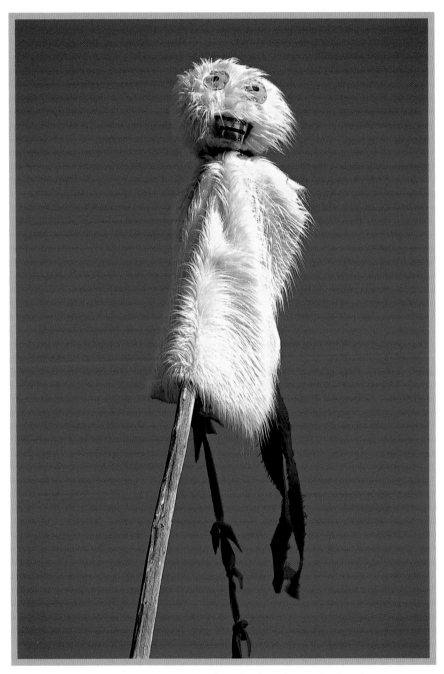

Figures sacred to the Mandan were often displayed outside their homes.

the souls of the bravest men went to the villages of the gods. Sometimes, a soul went to the village of the wicked. Life in these villages was the same as that on earth. There, warriors went into battle and hunted and enjoyed an abundance of food.

Each person also believed that an animal, such as a buffalo, turtle, or frog, lived within him. Women believed that they had an ear of corn inside that appeared when they danced.

The mysteries of nature were blended into Mandan beliefs. For example, the glittering eyes of Thunderbird caused lightning as he dug a path through the black storm clouds for the rain. The Mandan believed that isolated thunderclaps were caused by an enormous turtle living in the clouds. The Rainbow, a spirit that accompanied the Sun, came out when the Sun hid behind the clouds. The aurora borealis, or northern lights, was believed to be a fire kindled by a gathering of the medicine men and the warriors of northern tribes who were cooking their dead enemies in large pots. Like their Sioux neighbors, the Mandan believed that each star was a person. When a child was born, the star descended to earth and lived in that person. When that person died, the star returned to the night sky. The Mandan believed that many supernatural beings dwelled among the stars.

The Mandan believed deeply in the power of dreams to guide their daily actions. People also thought that everyday situations influenced fortune. For example, people believed that the presence of a pregnant woman brought good luck to the game of *tchung-kee* but bad luck to her husband when he

Lone Man taught the Mandan how to make a fire.

was hunting. People followed many customs to assure prosperity. They built a fire as Lone Man had instructed them—with two sticks crossed at the center. They gradually pushed the sticks in toward the flame as they burned. Lone Man also taught the Mandan how to kill buffalo, make shields, tattoo themselves, and undertake many other activities, all of which were held sacred.

Throughout their lives, people frequently underwent penances and sacrifices. From an early age, children were encouraged to seek spiritual power through fasting, torturing themselves, and giving away their possessions, especially during the Okipa ceremony. They might even cut off a finger joint as an offering. After three or four days of fasting and self-torture, they acquired a medicine spirit who served as a personal guardian. Often assuming the form of an animal, the medicine spirit appeared to the person in a dream. No hunting, battle, or expedition was ever undertaken without calling upon a supernatural being for help. People fasted and prayed for a day or more by one of the village's sacred structures known as medicine scaffolds.

The Mandan had many shrines, such as the Ark, or Big Canoe, on the main plaza of the village around which ceremonies were held. There was also a shrine on one side of the plaza. This shrine was made of four poles and had soil and sod heaped around the base of the two front poles. Four buffalo skulls were placed between the front poles and twenty-six human skulls painted with red stripes were arranged by the back poles. Sometimes, figures representing the Sun and the Moon or First Creator and the Old Woman Who Never Dies were tied to the poles. A figure of Ochkih-Hadda made of skin and sticks hung in the medicine lodge. Similar figures of First Creator and Lone Man were displayed in the other lodges.

The most important shrine was the medicine rock located atop a hill about a two- or three-day journey from the villages. People believed that the rock could predict the future. They visited it every spring and sometimes during the summer. They consulted the rock regarding key decisions, such as whether to go to war. The Mandan also greatly respected a lake in which they believed there lived a wise and powerful serpent

This painting by Karl Bodmer shows a Mandan man standing beside a shrine.

that was once a great warrior. People often traveled to the lake, threw offerings into the water, and asked the serpent for help.

The most revered objects of the Mandan were the sacred bundles, kept by the tribe, clans, and individuals. Every person had his or her own sacred bundle, the contents of which were kept secret from others. These sacred bundles were hung outside the doorways of earth lodges. People relied on their own sacred bundles to treat illnesses and injuries. If these did not prove effective, they called in a doctor who held rights to the tribe's sacred bundles. Both male and female doctors could purchase these rights or acquire them through visions. There was also a large sacred bundle in the medicine lodge.

Certain animals were considered sacred by the Mandan. Owls were kept in lodges because people believed they could predict the future. They revered eagles and hawks, and these birds of prey were captured for their feathers. The Mandan believed geese were sacred because in one story First Creator had turned into a goose and flown away with a flock. Geese were also thought to be messengers for the Old Woman Who Never Dies. The most sacred animal was the white buffalo. The robes of these rare animals were the most valuable possessions of the Mandan. Often purchased from other tribes, the hides of white buffalo were tanned with the hooves and horns left on. A white buffalo robe was worth ten to fifteen horses or sixty ordinary buffalo robes. No man could achieve a high position in the village if he did not own at least one white buffalo robe. After a man acquired a white buffalo robe, an elaborate ceremony was held by the shaman, or healer.

Ceremonies

The Mandan had many different ceremonies. Some expressed their religious beliefs in a general way, while others had a single purpose, such as the consecration of a new pipe, gun, or horse. There were two kinds of dances: those in which everyone could participate and those in which only members of the societies could take part. Two of the most important were the Buffalo Dance, which was held to encourage herds of buffalo to come near the villages, and the Corn Dance in which prayers and offerings were made to the corn spirit. Men who had recently won honor in battle held a Scalp Dance. Other ceremonies revolved around such important activities as eagle trapping or the preparation of sacred bundles.

The most important religious ceremony for women centered around corn, especially at planting time, and involved prayers, songs, and chants. A group known as the Goose Woman Society managed the planting, cultivation, and harvest of the corn, along with ceremonies to ensure a bountiful crop. The Old Woman Who Never Dies, or the Corn Mother, was a key figure in farming ceremonies.

The Mandan's most significant religious ceremony, the Okipa ceremony, was undertaken to ensure plentiful harvests and abundant buffalo. This four-day ritual included dances, prayers, and offerings to the spirits, especially the sun. Corn and buffalo were the key symbols. In this complex and colorful ceremony,

This painting shows Mandan women dancing.

the Mandan recounted the creation of the world, including the plants, animals, and people. In theatrical, costumed reenactments, they dramatized the struggle of their people to achieve their place in the order of the universe. Men who had inherited or purchased the rights to songs, chants, and rituals took part in the Okipa ceremony. Participants sought not only prosperity for the village but also slipped into trances in which they communicated with the spirits. The Mandan renewed themselves through the Okipa ceremony.

Making their home on the northern plains where the winters are bitterly cold and game is often scarce, the Mandan also relied on spirits to guide them through times of peril. These spirits brought many useful tools and skills to the Mandan, which helped people survive the hard winters and better understand their place in the universe. The good works of these spirits were often recalled in stories, which are still enjoyed today. Children love to gather around elders to listen to these stories, which instruct the young of each generation about the beliefs and customs of the Mandan.

Here is a story about Corn Silk and Split Feather and how they came to help the people:

There once was a young woman named Corn Silk, who was so beautiful that all the young men of the Mandan villages wished to marry her. However, she refused every one of them.

As time went by, her brothers became impatient and told her, "We want you to marry Split Feather, who lives in the far north."

The young woman thought about their suggestion and said to herself, "Since my brothers wish me to marry this man, I will do so."

Before she went on her journey to find Split Feather, she roasted and pounded corn, which she mixed with ground sunflower seeds and other ingredients to make the corn balls known as "four-in-one." With the corn balls and some dried meat, she set out early the next morning and traveled all day.

That evening, she came to a dwelling of sticks and grass near the edge of the timber. Inside, several women were talking about their crops. When a child was sent for water, the women noticed Corn Silk and asked, "Who is standing outside?"

"It is Corn Silk," she answered.

The women, who were mouse people with whitish hair on their bellies, invited her into their home. Corn Silk shared the corn balls and dried meat with them.

One of the women asked, "Where are you going?"

Corn Silk answered, "I am journeying north to marry Split Feather."

"It is a dangerous journey," the women told her. "But tomorrow you will come to your grandfather's house. The people there will do their best to protect you. We will also try to help you."

The next day, Corn Silk left and traveled all day until she came to a dwelling similar to that of the women. The mouse people with black skin lived here. As Corn Silk stood by the door, she heard people talking. When one of them sent a child for firewood, they noticed her and asked in fright, "Who is at the door?"

"It is Corn Silk," she answered.

The mouse people invited her inside and prepared an evening meal of roots and herbs, along with her corn balls and dried meat. They asked Corn Silk where she was going, and she told them, "I am on my way to marry Split Feather, who lives in the far north."

They cried out, "He is a terrible person! But we will try to help you. You will next come to your grandmother's camp. Whatever they tell you will be useful to you."

The next day, Corn Silk left and arrived in the evening at the grandmother's camp where the mole people lived under the ground. They visited with Corn Silk and on the following day guided her to the badger people, who also made their home beneath the soil. All the badger people were so old they had white hair. They told Corn Silk, "You will come to Split Feather's home tomorrow, and he will try to kill you. So before you arrive, you must tie strings to your moccasins, bracelets, and necklaces. Split Feather will take you to a stream where the fish have sharp teeth and make you stand on a buffalo skull. He will turn into a golden eagle and fly up into the air. You must then kick the buffalo skull into the stream and throw yourself on the ground. We will then be able to help you."

The next day Corn Silk was frightened when she arrived at the home of Split Feather. She spent the night there, and the next morning Split Feather said, "Let us bathe in the stream."

Corn Silk went with Split Feather to the stream with high banks on either side. Standing on the edge of the steep bank, Split Feather prayed to the spirits, "I have made many offerings to you, but this is to be the finest gift."

As he spoke, the fish jumped furiously in the water.

Split Feather ordered Corn Silk to stand on the buffalo skull and then he left. Glancing back, Corn Silk noticed that he had turned into a golden eagle. As the badger people had instructed her, she quickly kicked the buffalo skull into the water and the fish rose to devour it. Corn Silk then flung herself onto the ground. Split Feather swooped down upon her and tried to throw her into the stream. However, the underground people tightly grasped the strings tied to her moccasins, bracelets, and necklaces. Split Feather could not move her. When he flew up into the sky, the underground people told Corn Silk, "Snatch away his necklace. It is his heart." And when Split Feather swooped down again, she seized the necklace. Split Feather instantly became a human being.

He begged her to give back the necklace, but she refused. They returned to his lodge. Since she had the necklace, which was his heart, she soon gained his love. They lived happily together for many years and had one child.

During this time, Corn Silk found that she could transform herself into corn, just as Split Feather could become an eagle. Learning that her people desperately needed corn, she suggested that they return to her village. Corn Silk and Split Feather could then journey back and forth between the two homes.

Split Feather readily agreed. So they set off and arrived at her village late at night. The door was fastened, so Corn Silk called out and someone within the lodge said to her father, "That is the voice of your daughter."

The old man opened the door and there stood his daughter with her husband and son. Corn Silk and her father hugged each other joyfully.

Since everyone was very hungry, Corn Silk immediately told the people to clean their pit cellars. She then asked the owner of each pit what variety of corn was usually stored there—white, yellow, blue, or some other kind. When the owner told her, Corn Silk dropped a few kernels of that corn into the pit. If the owner opened the pit the next day, she found that it was one-quarter filled. If she waited two days, the pit was half filled and after three days it was three-quarters full. If she patiently waited four days, the pit was full to the brim. The people rejoiced. And since that day when Corn Silk came back to them, they have been very successful in growing many kinds of corn.

One day, Corn Silk, Split Feather, and their son went down to the river. While Corn Silk and Split Feather bathed in the water, their son found the necklace in the secret place where Corn Silk had long ago sewed it into her robe. Both Corn Silk and Split Feather saw the necklace and rushed up the bank. Arriving first, Split Feather seized the necklace and put it on. Immediately, he became a golden eagle again. He said, "My people are hungry, and I am going back to my home in the north. Our child will grow into a man and become a leader of his people who will always be taken care of." He named the child Looks-Down-On-the-Ground-From-Above.

And so it was. Thereafter, through the help of Corn Silk, Split Feather, and their son, who soon became a man, the Mandan prospered.

Many stories like this were used to explain the relationship between people and the earth they lived on. These stories explained weather patterns and why a harvest was better one year than the next, and also gave the tribe guidelines for how to treat one another. These stories are unique to the Mandan peoples, but the role of religion in a culture is universal. Throughout history, humans have tried to understand the world they live in and their role in it.

The Mandan decorated robes with colorful designs and detailed images.

Beliefs of the Mandan

Europeans forever changed Native American ways of life.

CHAPTER FIVE

*I do not fear death,
my friends.*

—Four Bears, 1800–1837

OVERCOMING HARDSHIPS

Today the Three Affiliated Tribes include the Mandan, Hidatsa, and Arikara, but for centuries these groups thrived independently in their villages along the northern rivers. There were key differences that separated these groups, including customs and language. The Mandan and Hidatsa spoke Siouan languages, while the Arikara were members of the **Caddoan** language group. The populations of these tribes were so large in the 1700s, before the arrival of Europeans and smallpox epidemics that killed Natives at an alarming rate, that even a single tribe had multiple settlements. The Hidatsa lived in three villages at the mouth of the Knife River, north of the present-day town of Stanton, North Dakota. The Mandan had nine villages near the mouth of the Heart River near what is now the city of Mandan, North Dakota. The Arikara lived in central South Dakota. Some of their villages extended into the northwestern part of the state into an area known as Grand River.

Coming Together

Even before contact with people of European descent, all three tribes were gradually migrating upriver. In the late 1700s, their migrations became more frantic as each tribe—especially the Mandan—was ravaged by smallpox epidemics. By the early 1800s, the Mandan had moved to within a few miles of the Hidatsa villages.

The Hidatsa dominated the hunting on the northern plains, while the Arikara controlled the southern region. Both the Mandan and the Hidatsa excelled as farmers and traders on the northern plains. Their trade network extended to the Southwest and Mexico, and the Arikara served as middlemen, especially in trading for corn. They also traded hides and meat. From the Assiniboine the three tribes acquired guns and horses.

After a major smallpox epidemic in 1837, the Mandan were so reduced that they could no longer survive as an independent tribe. The Mandan abandoned their villages and migrated with the Hidatsa for several years. The Hidatsa were also devastated, but many tribal members who were hunting buffalo on the prairies managed to elude the disease. Meanwhile, the

Arikara, who had been increasingly pressured by the advance of the Sioux, decided to leave their villages. They moved into the earth lodges left by the Mandan. The Mandan and the Hidatsa established Like-a-Fishhook Village on a scenic bend of the Missouri River. Since the 1790s, explorers had traversed this area, and in the early 1800s, the Lewis and Clark expedition passed through this region on their journey up the Missouri River. It was there, in 1845, that Bartholomew Berthold established Fort Berthold, an American Fur Company post.

The **Treaty** of Fort Laramie of 1851 established the boundary of a reservation for the Hidatsa, Mandan, and Arikara. In 1870, the Fort Berthold Reservation was established, and a year later the Mandan, Hidatsa, and Arikara were formally situated on the reservation. In the process, their land holdings were reduced, but neither Congress nor the tribal members ever agreed to this loss of land. In 1890, the tribes lost more land when the Northern Pacific Railroad was given the southern half of the reservation to finance construction of a rail line.

As people moved into communities scattered over the reservation, the population of Like-a-Fishhook Village gradually dwindled. The community was abandoned in 1888. Then, in 1891, the Dawes Allotment Act divided the reservation into 160-acre (64.7 ha) parcels. Although families now held individual parcels of land, tribal members managed to maintain a sense of clan and community. About two-thirds of the remaining reservation lands were sold to non-Natives. In 1910, the northeastern corner of the reservation

The Garrison Dam has a notorious history with the Mandan tribe, starting with the dam's completion in 1954.

The People and Culture of the Mandan

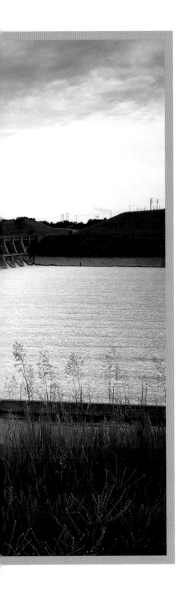

was seized and sold to settlers. Over the years, the size of the reservation was gradually reduced, from about 13,500,000 acres (5,463,256 ha) to around 900,000 acres (364,217 ha).

In 1948, the Three Affiliated Tribes of Fort Berthold Reservation were forced to sell 155,000 acres (62,726 ha) of their land to make way for the construction of the Garrison Dam and **Reservoir**. At the signing of the papers with the US Secretary of the Interior, George Gillette, the council chairman of the reservation remarked, "The members of the tribal council sign this contract with heavy hearts. Right now, the future does not look so good to us. Our Treaty of Fort Laramie made in 1851, our tribal constitution, are being torn to shreds."

In 1954, when the US Army Corps of Engineers completed Garrison Dam and Reservoir, the rising waters flooded large areas of fertile bottomland. Nearly all of the tribal members lived in the bottomlands on farms and in villages. The villages were now covered by water. Roads vanished, leaving people on the reservation separated into five isolated areas. People were relocated from the farms and woods of the bottomlands to the dry, windswept prairies. In subsequent hearings, one tribal member described the higher location as a "treeless, farmless, waterless, foreign land." Many people, along with the tribal government, were moved to the aptly named community of New Town. Over the years, other small communities—notably White Shield, Mandaree, and Twin Buttes—have been established, but many people still miss their old homes. No efforts were made to rebuild the flooded villages, and many people found themselves isolated on family homesteads scattered throughout the reservation. The bonds of clan and community were broken, and many people ended up leaving the reservation. However, as Cora Baker reflected later in 1984, "We had no choice, I guess, just like a gopher, you know, when they pour water in your house you better get out or drown."

To this day, tribal members mourn the loss of their land. In the words of Gerald Baker, "Today I can only go to Independence Point, look over the thousands of acres of water and try to imagine what it was like. My thoughts are usually interrupted by speedboats, pleasure boats, and fishermen who are usually non-Indians enjoying the lake, not knowing or caring about the history that lies underneath the waters."

Mandan Language

The Mandan language belongs in the Siouan family of languages and is most closely related to the speech of the Hidatsa and the Crow. Within the tribe there are three dialects: Nuptadi, Nuitadi, and Awigaxa.

The language has nearly been lost. As of 1992, only six people spoke Mandan. However, efforts are being made to save the language, with courses now taught at Fort Berthold Community College on the reservation, as well as through the MHA Summer Institute in New Town, North Dakota. The MHA Summer Institute offers classes specific to Mandan, Hidatsa, and Arikara. These classes are for the community and also help teachers in the area perfect their skills so they can teach in the schools.

The following examples are based on a list compiled by H. J. Spinden and G. F. Will and published in *The Mandans: a Study of the Culture, Archaeology, and Language*. Mandan is a complicated language, but the key and examples should be helpful for the pronunciation of most words.

Vowels are generally pronounced as follows:

a	as in father
e	as in met
i	as in machine
ô	as in not
o	as in note
u	as in boot

The consonants are generally pronounced as in English, except for the glottal stop. This is a catch in the throat, as in the slight pause between uh oh! A glottal stop is indicated by a ' before the consonant.

Below are some everyday words used by the Mandan.

People

sukxamahe	baby
suknumank	boy
mo'ka	brother
tate	father
manuka	friend
sukmihe	girl
tatecike	grandfather
nancike	grandmother
umank	man
hu'de	mother
tamixena	sister
mihe	woman

Body Parts

ahde	arms
nakoha	ears
akcicenahde	elbow
ista	eyes
estah	face
unkahe	fingers
ci	foot
pahin	hair
onka	hand
pan	head
natka	heart
dohka	leg
ihe	mouth

pahu	nose
akit	shoulder

Natural World

haade	cloud
beddede	dew
istamenahke	moon
xeduc	rain
xehikuhnde	rainbow
passahe, passa'he	river
wahe	snow
manaininduc	tree
owakope	valley
mini	water

Animals

koka	antelope
patake	bald eagle
mahto	bear
warahpa	beaver
a'saxte	bighorn sheep
mandek	bird
ptemde	buffalo
mahmanaku	deer
menisswarut	dog
patohe	duck
ompa	elk
po	fish
psanka	frog
miha'kcuke	goose, wild

meniss, umpameniss	horse
pahi	porcupine
sipuska	prairie chicken
maxtike	rabbit

There is a long history of the Mandan people adapting to new languages, however. The plains tribes (sometimes called the Plains Indians) also used a special sign language called **Plains Indian Sign Language (PISL)**, which allowed the different tribes to communicate and negotiate without speaking. Western visitors were so impressed with the Natives' ability to communicate silently that one Spanish explorer said they were "so skillful in the use of signs that it seemed as if they spoke." Today, after years of accommodating other languages, the tribes are returning to their native tongue in order to keep their culture alive.

Native American communities, including the Mandan, have their own form of sign language. Here, a woman makes a sign for beauty.

A boy dances at a powwow on the Fort Berthold Reservation in 2014.

*[Those with a] good heart
will enter the Okipa Lodge.
They must have the genuine
love of mankind, and they
must have humility.*

—Mandan saying

THE NATION'S PRESENCE NOW

Today, the Fort Berthold Reservation is home to many Mandan, Hidatsa, and Arikara people. These three tribes were formally united as the Three Affiliated Tribes under laws outlined in the Indian Reorganization Act of June 18, 1934. The tribal government now operates under a constitution and bylaws approved on June 28, 1936, and a Federal

This crest shows the Three Affiliated Tribes, which was created with the signing of the Fort Laramie Treat of 1851.

Corporation Charter ratified on April 23, 1937. Both documents have since been amended.

Jobs and Education

The sprawling reservation encompasses about 980,000 acres (396,591 ha), with about half the land owned by non-Natives. Most Mandan now live on the west side of the reservation near the town of Twin Buttes. Total enrollment, or membership, for all three tribes is over ten thousand people. About 4,060 live on the reservation. Most people on the reservation are employed by federal and tribal agencies. The Three Affiliated Tribes opened a gambling casino in 1993

Casinos such as Four Bears Casino and Resort Hotel help bolster economy on the Fort Berthold Reservation.

to provide jobs, but unemployment still remains high. Later, a tourist complex was added to strengthen the economy, as well as to teach tourists about the tribes. Drilling for oil has also provided additional jobs and income, but at a cost. An oil spill of three thousand barrels in 2014 contaminated a large portion of the reservation's land. It has also created a divide between tribe members who have made lots of money from

The Three Affiliate Tribal Museum houses displays and artifacts explaining the Three Affiliated Tribes' history.

the oil and those who have seen little benefit. Through the school system and social services, the tribal government is striving to provide the education and job skills that people will need for economic prosperity in the twenty-first century.

Maintaining Traditions

As they struggle with the challenges of economic growth on the reservation and contemporary life in the United States, the Mandan, along with the Hidatsa and the Arikara, are committed to maintaining their traditional culture and history. Many artisans make finely crafted items of beadwork and quillwork. The tribes publish a newspaper called the *Mandan, Hidatsa and Arikara Times*. The reservation has a museum at New Town, and several communities hold powwows during the summer months. Ceremonies known as Warbonnet Dances help to strength people's identity as Native Americans. A warbonnet is a headdress. Modern Warbonnet Dances are sometimes performed to honor members of the community who have died while

Today the Mandan preserve their past through reconstructed villages, traditional housing such as tipis, tribal events, celebrations, and language.

serving in the US military or some other significant event in the community.

The traditional Okipa ceremony is a very important event in the Mandan tribe, but after smallpox infected their villages and wiped out most of the population, the Mandan performed their last Okipa in 1889. That is, until 2011, when Cedric Red Feather led the first Okipa in 122 years. Unlike the Okipas of the past, Red Feather did not encourage tribe members to torture themselves but to be open and generous with one another.

Although only a few elders speak Mandan, the language is now taught in the schools. In recent years, linguists from Yale have worked with tribe members to develop textbooks so the language can be taught widely, and programs like the MHA (Mandan, Hidatsa, Arikara) Language Project offer summer intensive courses at the Nueta Hidatsa Sahnish College in New Town, North Dakota. Through the efforts of individuals and tribal organizations, the Mandan have been able to preserve much of their past, even as they prepare for a better future.

Crow's Heart was a member of the Mandan tribe. Here he wears traditional clothing.

CHAPTER SEVEN

We need strong leadership to make sure our rights ... our trust lands are always protected and to see that our sovreignty is protected and enhanced.

—Tex Hall, former tribal chairman

FACES OF THE MANDAN

Over the centuries, the Mandan tribe has relied on their clan leaders to make decisions about the tribe's migration, negotiated with visitors, and officiated religious ceremonies. Over time, the role of these leaders has evolved to meet the demands of the changing world around them. Today, for example, some of the most important leaders are those who are active in the community and advocate for equal rights and education for their tribe members.

Cedric Red Feather (1949–) is an artist and Turtle Priest. In the Mandan tribe, the Turtle Priest gains the responsibility at birth to carry the stories and history of the people to future generations. Red Feather brought attention back to the tribe's history when in 2011 he led the first Okipa in 122 years. He has also written a book, Mandan Dreams, about the oral history, **prophecy**, and traditions of the Mandan.

This illustration shows Mato-Tope in full regalia.

The People and Culture of the Mandan

Mato-Tope (Four Bears) (1800–1837) was chief of a Mandan village near the Big Bend of the upper Missouri River. He welcomed early explorers and traders to the region. In the winter of 1804–1805, the Lewis and Clark expedition stayed with Mato-Tope and his people.

In 1832, artist George Catlin visited the Mandan. In 1834, artist Karl Bodmer arrived with Prince Maximilian zu Wied's expedition. The two men made many sketches and paintings of the Mandan, including several portraits of Mato-Tope. The chief presented Catlin and Bodmer with examples of his own artwork on buffalo robes and paper. One drawing shows a battle scene in which both Mato-Tope and a Cheyenne chief were wounded.

In 1837, Mato-Tope was chosen as chief of his village. The same year, however, he died in the smallpox epidemic.

Sheheke (Big White) (circa 1765–ca. 1815) was chief of the lower village of Mitutahank near the confluence of the Knife and Missouri Rivers. During the winter of 1804–1805, he provided food and shelter to the Lewis and Clark expedition. Sheheke also generously shared his knowledge of people, animals, and plants on the northern plains, which helped the explorers in mapping and learning about the territory.

When the expedition returned eighteen months later, Lewis invited Sheheke to Washington, DC. The chief agreed, provided he could bring his wife and children, as well as his interpreter René Jusseaume and his family. Sheheke visited in Washington and

SHA-HA-KA
A MANDAN CHIEF.

A portrait of Sheheke

The People and Culture of the Mandan

Philadelphia, where French artist Charles Balthasar Julien Févre de Saint-Mémin painted his portrait. During his journey, Sheheke visited President Thomas Jefferson's home at Monticello to view his collection of Native American artifacts.

Sheheke's return trip was delayed because of hostilities among the tribes living on the upper Missouri, in which Jusseaume was wounded. Journeying up the Missouri River under the protection of the Missouri Fur Company, the chief finally returned home in September 1809. Sheheke never regained his stature in the village because people never believed his stories about his trip to the East. Years later, he died in a battle with the Sioux.

Tillie Walker (1928–) was born and raised on the reservation of the Three Affiliated Tribes at Fort Berthold, North Dakota. As she grew up, Walker became very concerned about the welfare of the Mandan and other Native peoples. Over the years, she has devoted herself to improving the quality of life for Native Americans, especially for young people. She has been most actively involved in the American Friends Service Committee, the United Scholarship Service (founded to assist Native American and Spanish American college students), and the Indian Rights Association on whose board she also served. In August 1961, as a staff member of the American Friends Service Committee, Walker helped establish the National Indian Youth Council (NIYC) in Gallup, New Mexico. In 2014, Walker and her sister Reba purchased a large portion of land neighboring the Berthold

Tillie Walker (*second from the left*) and friends let their voices ring out, 1970.

reservation to return to the Three Affiliated Tribes. This land once belonged to the tribes and represented to them an important return.

Kathy Whitman (Elk Woman) (1952–), Mandan-Hidatsa-Arikara, was born in Bismarck, North Dakota. She attended Standing Rock Community College in Fort Yates, North Dakota, and the University of South Dakota from 1973 to 1978. She became a teacher and artist who sculpts in stone and paints in oils. Best known for her sculptures, she has exhibited her work at the National Museum of the American Indian in

The People and Culture of the Mandan

New York City and the Heard Museum in Phoenix, Arizona. She has also exhibited at the Western Museum in Medora, North Dakota; the Sioux Indian Museum and Craft Center in Rapid City, South Dakota; the Five Civilized Tribes Museum in Muskogee, Oklahoma; and many other museums and galleries. She won first prize at the annual Trail of Tears Art Show at the Cherokee National Museum, Tahlequah, Oklahoma, in 1987 and 1990. Whitman has won best-of-show awards and first prizes at several other art exhibitions.

Kathy Whitman

A young Mandan woman takes in the landscape, wearing ceremonial clothes.

In the Three Affiliated Tribes community, everyone plays a valuable role in the lives of the tribe members. From the chief to the artists who spread the culture and traditions of the tribespeople, many influential figures have participated in the Mandan's rich history.

CHRONOLOGY

1738 French explorer Pierre de Vérendrye is the first person of European descent to visit Mandan villages on the Missouri River.

1742 Vérendrye's sons return to North Dakota to continue their father's quest for a northwest passage to the Pacific Ocean.

1781 Smallpox epidemic nearly wipes out the entire Mandan population. Just two of nine villages are left. The Mandan move from the Heart to the Knife River.

1790 Jacques d'Eglise, a Saint Louis trader, journeys to Mandan villages on behalf of Spain.

1792 The Arikara move up the Missouri River and settle near the Cannonball River.

1794–1796 René Jusseaume establishes a post for the North West Company in North Dakota.

1797 David Thompson, an English geographer, explores the basins of the Mouse and Missouri Rivers. The first fur trading post of the North West Company is established on Park River.

1800 The French get Louisiana back from the Spanish but sell the territory to the United States in 1803.

1804–1806 Lewis and Clark winter at Fort Mandan in 1804, journey to the Pacific Ocean, and return in 1806 on their way back to Saint Louis.

1809 Manuel Lisa travels from Saint Louis for the Missouri Fur Company and establishes Fort Manuel Lisa on the west side of the Missouri River.

1818 By treaty, the United States acquires the eastern edge of what would become North Dakota from Great Britain.

1837 Smallpox epidemic sweeps through the Mandan villages, reducing the population from around 1,600 to about 135 people.

1845 Bartholomew Berthold establishes Fort Berthold, an American Fur Company post on the Missouri River. The Mandan join the Hidatsa at Like-a-Fishhook Village.

1870 Fort Berthold Reservation is established.

1871 Mandan and Hidatsa are situated on the Fort Berthold Reservation.

1888 Like-a-Fishhook Village is abandoned.

1934 Indian Reorganization Act formally recognizes the political union of the Mandan, Arikara, and Hidatsa as the Three Affiliated Tribes.

1951–1954 Mandan are relocated when the Garrison Dam and Reservoir are constructed.

2011 First Okipa ceremony held since 1889.

2014 Tribal elders Tillie and Reba Walker donate their family land back to the Three Affiliated Tribes.

GLOSSARY

affiliated Joined or associated.

agrarian society A group of people who rely on farming for food.

Caddoan A language family of the Great Plains, including Arikara and Pawnee.

count coup To tuch an enemy in battle. It is considered an act worthy of honor.

earth lodge A dwelling made of a wooden frame covered with layers of sod.

epidemic A widespread outbreak in which many people become ill.

expedition An organized journey, usually of a large party, for purposes of exploration.

Great Plains The flat grasslands between the Mississippi River and Rocky Mountains.

jerky Thin strips of meat preserved by drying in the sun.

Louisiana Purchase Land acquired by the United States from France in 1803 comprising territory west of the Mississippi River.

Okipa ceremony A four-day ceremony recounting the history of the Mandan Tribe.

parfleche A leather pouch or sheet used for storing food, clothing, and other belongings.

pemmican Dried, pounded meat mixed with fat and berries used by warriors as energy food on long journeys.

Plains Indian Sign Language (PISL) A form of sign language developed by the Native Plains Indians.

polytheistic Belief in and worship of more than one god.

prophecy A prediction of the future.

reservation A tract of land set aside by the government as a home for Native Americans.

reservoir An artificial lake that is formed behind a dam.

Siouan A language family spoken by many tribes living in eastern North America.

tipi Cone-shaped structure made of poles covered with animal skins.

travois Sled-like carrier made of two poles lashed to the sides of a dog or horse and dragged behind it.

treaty A signed, legal agreement between two nations.

BIBLIOGRAPHY

Fenn, Elizabeth A. *Encounters at the Heart of the World: A History of the Mandan People*. New York: Hill and Wang, 2015.

"The History and Culture of the Three Affiliated Tribes Government." Ndstudies.org. Accessed July 5, 2016. http://www.ndstudies.org/resources/IndianStudies/threeaffiliated/historical_overview.html.

"Mandan – Religion and Expressive Culture." *Countries and Their Cultures*. Accessed June 30, 2016. http://www.everyculture.com/North-America/Mandan-Religion-and-Expressive-Culture.html.

"MHA Nation - Mandan, Hidatsa & Arikara." *MHA Nation – Mandan, Hidatsa & Arikara*. Accessed June 29, 2016. http://www.mhanation.com.

"National Geographic: Lewis & Clark—Winter Among the Mandan." *National Geographic*. Accessed June 30, 2016. http://www.nationalgeographic.com/lewisandclark/journey_leg_5.html.

"Oral History of the Dakota Tribes." *Welch Dakota Papers*. Ed. Colonel A.B. Welch. Accessed July 3, 2016. http://www.welchdakotapapers.com.

Schatz, Amber. "Tribal Elders Donate Land Back to Three
    Affiliated Tribal Members." KX News, June 13, 2014.
    http://www.kxnet.com/story/25716839/tribal-elders-
    donate-land-back-to-three-affiliated-tribal-members?clie
    nttype=generic&mobilecgbypass.

"Tribal Perspectives." *Teaching American History in the
    Northwest.* The University of Montana. Accessed
    July 1, 2016. http://www.indian-ed.org/sti-videos/tribal-
    perspectives-on-american-history-vol-i.

"Young Linguist Goes Mandan." *The Language
    Conservancy.* Accessed July 6, 2016. http://www.
    languageconservancy.org/blog/2014/06/12/young-
    linguist-goes-mandan.

FURTHER INFORMATION

Want to know more about the Mandan? Check out these websites, videos, and organizations.

Websites

The Language Conservancy

http://www.languageconservancy.org

The Language Conservancy works to save endangered languages. Their website is a great tool to learn more about what languages are at risk of being lost and why it's so important to save them.

Mandan, Hidatsa, Arikara Affiliated Tribes

http://www.mhanation.com

This is the official website for the Mandan, Hidatsa, and Arikara Affiliated tribes. It is a good resource for recent events and news about the Three Affiliated Tribes.

The Metropolitan Museum of Art

http://www.metmuseum.org

The Met in New York City boasts an exhibit called Plains Indians, Artists of Earth and Sky. You can find images from this special collection on the museum's website.

Videos

Archaeological Dig Unearths New Facts about Mandan Indians in Bismarck

http://www.youtube.com/watch?v=Uu1lVDmBHL8

For decades, social scientists and archeologists believed that the history of the Mandan people had been lost after the smallpox epidemic that killed many of the tribe members. Recent archaeological digs, like the one in this video, have yielded new information.

Mandan Tribe Documentary

http://www.youtube.com/watch?v=Y_m15J1y6OE

This short documentary covers the history of the Mandan people and their traditions on the North Dakota plains.

Native Americans People of the Plains

http://www.youtube.com/watch?v=DtfwCljzg7g

Discovery Education created this half-hour special on the Native Americans of the Plains which shows early Native migrations across the United States as well as how early Native Americans lived.

Organizations

Arikara, Hidatsa, and Mandan Three Affiliated Tribes

404 Frontage Road
New Town, ND 58763
(701) 627-3503
http://www.mhanation.com

Knife River Indian Villages National Historic Site

564 County Road 37

Stanton, ND 58571

(701) 745-3309

http://www.nps.gov/knri

Mandan, Hidatsa, Arikara Summer Institute

220 8th Ave. N

New Town, North Dakota 58763

(701) 627-4738

http://www.mhasi.com

North Dakota Lewis & Clark Interpretive Center

2576 8th St. SW

Washburn, ND 58577

(701) 462-8535

http://www.fortmandan.com

INDEX

Page numbers in **boldface** are illustrations. Entries in **boldface** are glossary terms.

The People and Culture of the Mandan

ABOUT THE AUTHORS

Tatiana Ryckman is a writer, editor, and teacher. She holds a bachelor's degree in journalism and master's degree in creative writing. Other books by Ryckman include *Oprah Winfrey: Media Mogul and Philanthropist* from the Leading Women series; *Alexander Hamilton: First Secretary of the Treasury and an Author of the Federalist Papers*, part of the Great American Thinkers series; and a collection of short stories, *Twenty-Something*. When she is not writing, she enjoys reading and bicycling with friends in Austin, Texas.

Raymond Bial has published more than eighty books—most of them photography books—during his career. His photo-essays for children include *Corn Belt Harvest*, *Amish Home*, *Frontier Home*, *Shaker Home*, *The Underground Railroad*, *Portrait of a Farm Family*, *With Needle and Thread: A Book About Quilts*, *Mist Over the Mountains: Appalachia and Its People*, *Cajun Home*, and *Where Lincoln Walked*.

The emeritus director of a small college library in the Midwest, he lives with his wife and three children in Urbana, Illinois.

The People and Culture of the Mandan